STATE OF VERMONT
DEPARTMENT OF LIBRARIES
REGIONAL LIBRARY
RD 2   BOX 244
ST. JOHNSBURY, VT 05819

GIVEN BY THE STATE OF VERMONT
DEPARTMENT OF LIBRARIES

VERMONT DEPARTMENT OF LIBRARIES
CHILDREN'S BOOK EXHIBIT CENTER
MONTPELIER, VERMONT 05602

Leukemia
by Judy Monroe

CRESTWOOD HOUSE

New York
Collier Macmillan Canada
Toronto
Maxwell Macmillan International Publishing Group
New York   Oxford   Singapore   Sydney

LIBRARY OF CONGRESS CATALOGING-IN-PUBLICATION DATA

Monroe, Judy.
    The facts about leukemia / by Judy Monroe. — 1st ed.
      p.   cm. — (The Facts about series)
    Summary: Describes childhood leukemia, its symptoms, characteristics, and the history of its discovery. Examines the progress that has been made in treating the disease.
    ISBN 0-89686-532-0
    1. Leukemia—Juvenile literature. I. Title. II. Series: Facts about
RC643.M628   1990
616.99'419—dc20   90-33663
                                                                                                                 CIP
                                                                                                                  AC

PHOTO CREDITS

Cover: Journalism Services: (John Patsch)
DRK Photo: (Don and Pat Valenti) 4
Ellen B. Senisi: 7
Journalism Services: (SIU) 9; (Tim McCabe) 24;
  (Scott Wanner) 29
Peter Arnold, Inc.: (SIU) 12, 27
Devaney Stock Photos: 14; (Ann Ora Troxler) 18, 32, 34, 38;
  (Phyllis Sanders) 41
The Image Works: (Bob Daemmrich) 17;
  (Mark Antman) 22; (W. Marc Bernsau) 37

The publisher wishes to acknowledge the help of the Leukemia Society of America in the preparation of this book.

Copyright © 1990 by Crestwood House, Macmillan Publishing Company

All rights reserved. No part of this book may be reproduced or transmitted in any form or by any means, electronic or mechanical, including photocopying, recording, or by any information storage and retrieval system, without permission in writing from the Publisher.

Macmillan Publishing Company
866 Third Avenue
New York, NY 10022

Collier Macmillan Canada, Inc.
1200 Eglinton Avenue East
Suite 200
Don Mills, Ontario M3C 3N1

Printed in the United States of America
First Edition
10 9 8 7 6 5 4 3 2 1

CONTENTS

Leukemia Progress 5
Who Gets Leukemia? 6
White Blood 8
Your Blood 9
What Happens in Leukemia? 11
Kinds of Childhood Leukemia 13
Causes of Leukemia 14
Warning Signs 16
Hard to Diagnose 21
Treatment 24
Supportive Therapy 28
Todd's Story 30
After Treatment 32
In Remission 35
A Positive Outlook 36
Help for Leukemia Patients 39
Hope for the Future 42
For More Information 44
Glossary/Index 45–48

LEUKEMIA PROGRESS

Douglas Maurer, age 15, thought he had the flu. He ached all over. His temperature stayed between 103 and 105 degrees for several days. Bed rest, lots of liquids, aspirin—nothing helped. Finally Mrs. Maurer took Douglas to Children's Hospital at Washington University Medical Center in St. Louis, Missouri.

After many tests, the doctors told Douglas he had leukemia. Douglas was scared. He knew that leukemia is a *cancer*. Leukemia is a cancer of the body parts that make blood. Cancer is a disease in which some cells of the body grow too fast and destroy healthy tissues and organs.

Over the next few days, Douglas had more tests and started *chemotherapy*, or treatment with *anticancer drugs*. The doctors told Douglas he would need chemotherapy for three years. During treatment, he might lose his hair for a while and gain weight. He might have other reactions, such as red or itchy skin, headaches, or chills.

Douglas worried even more. But his doctors told him to stop worrying and think about getting well. They told him that with treatment his chances of living a long, healthy life were good.

Without treatment, most leukemia patients would die within a year. At one time, they did. Today doctors have greater success in treating and curing childhood leukemia.

One warning sign of leukemia is a flu or cold that will not go away.

However, leukemia still kills more young people between the ages of two and fifteen than any other disease. Most of these young victims are between the ages of two and four. Doctors and others are working hard to understand the disease and to improve treatment.

Although leukemia strikes both adults and children, this book is about childhood leukemia. What are the warning signs? What happens during treatment? When was the disease first discovered? Can anyone get leukemia?

WHO GETS LEUKEMIA?

Childhood leukemia strikes one in 30,000 children under the age of 15. Both males and females have an equal chance of getting the disease.

In the United States, about 27,300 new cases of leukemia were diagnosed in 1989. Out of every 10,000 adults and children, one person had leukemia. When doctors make a *diagnosis*, they examine a person and study his or her symptoms to find out what is wrong.

Many people think leukemia is mainly a children's disease. Actually, it strikes many more adults than children. In 1989, 25,000 adults and 2,300 children got leukemia. That means ten times as many adults as children get the disease. More than half of all leukemia cases occur in people over the age of 60.

Although more adults than children get leukemia, it kills more young people between the ages of two and fifteen than any other disease.

Leukemia is a rare disease. It accounts for about 5 percent of all cancer cases. That means out of 100 people with cancer, 5 have leukemia.

WHITE BLOOD

In 1847 a German doctor, Rudolf Virchow, first used the word "leukemia" to describe a new disease. Leukemia is a Greek word that means white blood. His patient's blood had too many *white blood cells.*

A leukemia patient's blood looks no different to the naked eye than anyone else's blood. However, a leukemia patient's blood looks different when seen through a *microscope.* A microscope is an instrument that enlarges, or magnifies, objects. When doctors look at a leukemia patient's blood through a microscope, they may see too many white blood cells. Or they may see white blood cells that are abnormal.

We now know that blood with too many white blood cells is the problem in half of all leukemia cases. We also know that leukemia is not a cancer of the blood as Dr. Virchow thought. Leukemia is a cancer of the tissues that form blood.

Until recently, doctors did not have good ways to treat the disease. Many people died within a few months of getting leukemia. Others might live a few years. Since the 1970s, doctors have developed successful treatments. Much of their success has been built on their greater understanding of blood.

YOUR BLOOD

Blood is an organ. It is made in the *bone marrow*. The bone marrow is a jellylike substance that fills the insides of bones. Blood supplies food, oxygen, and chemicals to all the body's cells. It removes carbon dioxide and other waste products and helps the *lymphatic system* fight infection.

The bone marrow constantly renews and replaces blood cells in an orderly way. All blood cells go through several growth stages until they mature. They are programmed to go through these stages.

This photo of a leukemia patient's blood under a microscope shows an abnormal number of white blood cells.

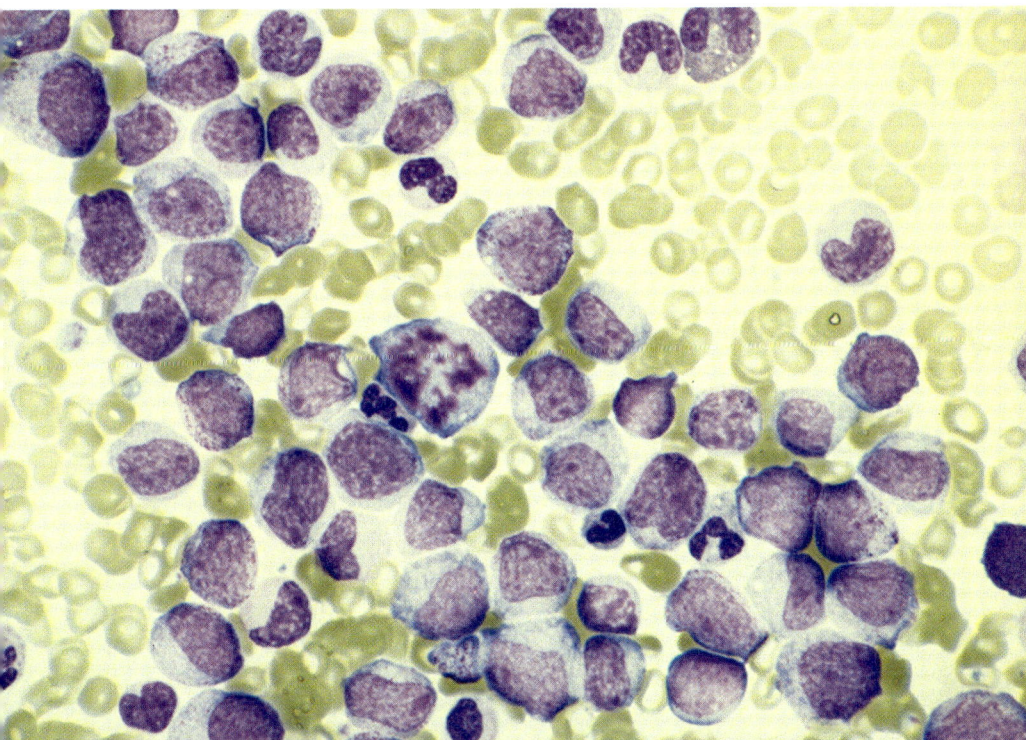

The bone marrow makes three kinds of cells. One is the *red blood cell*. Red blood cells give blood its red color. They also carry oxygen to all of the body's other tissues. The *platelets* are another type of cell. They help stop bleeding from an injury. The third type, white blood cells, fights infections.

Leukemia is a disease of the blood-forming tissues such as bone marrow, *spleen*, or *lymph nodes*. In leukemia, some white blood cells do not go through their normal growth stages. This can happen to any of three main kinds of white blood cells. These are the *neutrophils*, which "eat" *bacteria*; *monocytes*, which destroy foreign materials; and *lymphocytes*. Lymphocytes make substances to fight foreign materials.

When doctors speak about leukemia, they use the word *blast*. This is a short name for *lymphoblast*, the immature, or young, white blood cell. Normal blasts grow to form mature white blood cells that can fight infections. Leukemic blasts do not. Instead of aging and fighting infections, they remain young and multiply. They destroy the balance of all blood cells.

Sally is healthy. Her blood has the right balance of red and white blood cells and platelets. Blasts make up less than 5 percent of her blood.

Stan, age 10, has leukemia. His blood has incorrect numbers of platelets and red and white blood cells. His leukemic blasts are abnormal and do not look like healthy blasts. These blasts remain immature and cannot fight infections.

WHAT HAPPENS IN LEUKEMIA?

When a large number of blasts appear in the bone marrow, several things happen. More leukemic blast cells stay in the bone marrow. They begin crowding out normal cells. Over time, the leukemic blasts take up a lot of room. The red blood cells, platelets, and normal white blood cells cannot be produced. When this happens, leukemic blood looks different from normal blood. There are too many young blood cells in the bone marrow and not enough mature blood cells.

Tony's leukemic cells are crowding out his red blood cells. Doctors say his blood looks "thin." Roger's leukemia is different. Doctors do not find the right numbers of platelets in his bone marrow.

Joan, age 11, also has leukemia. Leukemic blasts are crowding out her normal white blood cells. When doctors look at her bone marrow, they see many blasts. They do not find enough older white blood cells.

Leukemic blasts sometimes spill over from the bone marrow into the blood. When doctors look at this blood through a microscope, they can spot these blasts. They may also see larger numbers of normal white cells in the blood. In Mary's kind of leukemia, her white cell count has increased. Although the

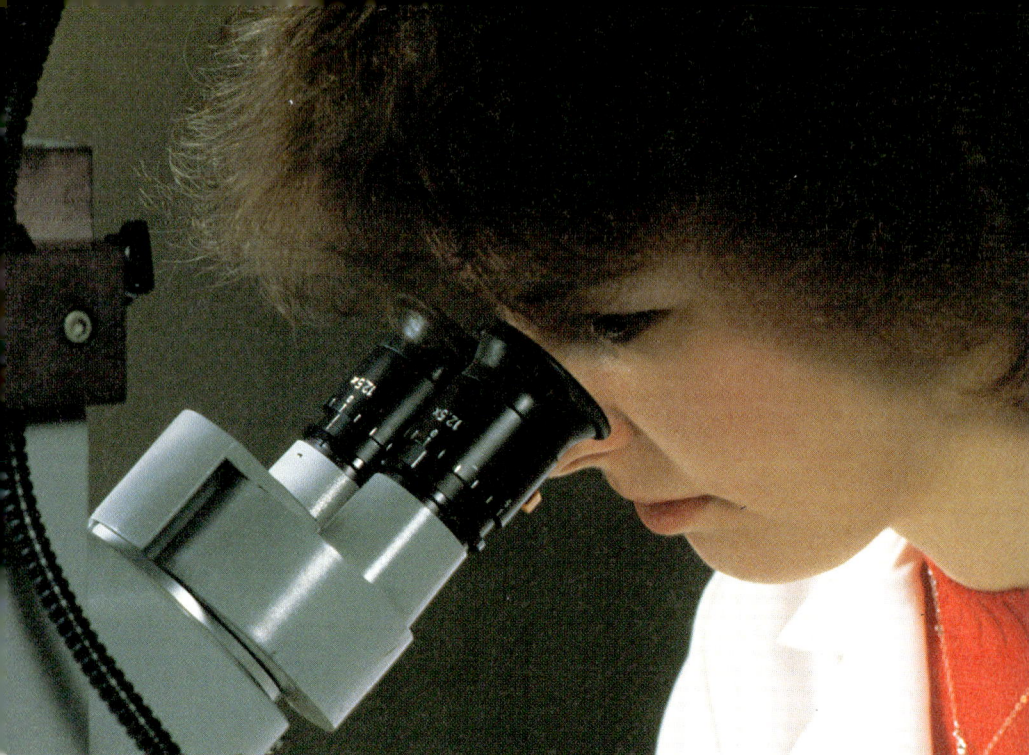

Doctors use special microscopes to locate blasts, the immature white blood cells found in leukemia patients.

leukemias of Tony, Roger, Joan, and Mary are different, they all have something in common. The disease developed quickly in each person.

Leukemic blasts in the blood may be carried to other places in the body. They may enter various body organs. Sometimes they will grow in these organs as well as in the bone marrow.

Leukemia itself rarely kills. Most often, young people may die from the spread of a minor infection. This is because their white blood cells can no longer fight off infection.

KINDS OF CHILDHOOD LEUKEMIA

Leukemia is not just one disease. There are three types of leukemia, one for each of the three major kinds of white blood cells—neutrophils, monocytes, and lymphocytes.

Leukemia usually affects only one kind of blood cell in each person. One kind of leukemia is lymphocytic. It affects the lymphocytes. Leukemias are different in the way they develop. Doctors divide them into two groups—*acute* and *chronic.*

Acute leukemia comes on quickly, sometimes in a few weeks. Ron, age 13, has acute leukemia. His disease would also progress rapidly if not treated. Acute leukemias account for 85 percent of the cases in young people.

The most common leukemia in children is *acute lymphocytic leukemia,* or ALL for short. It is often called childhood leukemia. Most children are two to eight years old when they get ALL. But the disease can occur in people in their 20s and 30s, too.

Slightly more boys than girls get ALL. It also occurs more often among white children than black children. Doctors do not know why.

In chronic leukemia, the bone marrow produces a good number of normal cells as well as leukemic cells.

Acute lymphocytic leukemia, the most common form of childhood leukemia, most often affects young white males.

So the disease is milder than acute leukemia and often develops more slowly.

Children seldom get chronic leukemia. Doctors can detect chronic leukemia from the large numbers of young neutrophil cells in the blood.

CAUSES OF LEUKEMIA

Causes of most leukemias are unknown. Some doctors think a *virus*, a tiny organism, causes the disease. Certain viruses cause leukemia in animals. However, researchers find that these viruses do not cause leukemia in people.

Researchers have discovered some unusual conditions that increase the risk of developing leukemia, however. Children with certain genetic problems such as Down's syndrome have a greater chance of getting leukemia. A few anticancer drugs and a workplace chemical called benzene may cause leukemia in a few adults. But they do not cause leukemia in children because children neither take these drugs nor are usually around benzene.

People exposed to very high amounts of radiation are more likely to develop leukemia. This was first shown in the 1920s. Back then, factory workers painted watch numbers with the element radium. The numbers glowed in the dark because radium is radioactive. Workers often licked their brush tips to get a fine point for painting. So some swallowed a lot of radium. Many of these workers developed leukemia.

Near the end of World War II, doctors again saw that high amounts of radiation caused leukemia. In 1945 the United States dropped atomic bombs on Hiroshima and Nagasaki, two cities in Japan. A large number of people in these cities soon developed leukemia.

A terrible accident in 1986 also resulted in higher-than-average numbers of leukemia cases. A nuclear power plant in Chernobyl, in the Soviet Union, did not function properly. An explosion happened that gave off intense amounts of radiation. Some people who were exposed to the radiation have developed leukemia, and more cases will probably occur.

Outside of these specific instances, doctors do not know what causes the disease. They know that nothing most children do—or do not do—causes leukemia. Childhood leukemia is not caused by any food, a fall, an injury, or X rays.

"I broke my arm and got X rays," said Ruth, age 13. "Can I get leukemia from the X rays? Or how about when I get my teeth X-rayed at the dentist?"

"Don't worry. Those are very small amounts of radiation," said her doctor. "They don't cause leukemia."

Children do not *inherit* leukemia from their parents. Beth, age 12, has leukemia. Her younger brother, Tom, is worried: "I'm her brother. Will I get it, too?"

"Just because your sister has leukemia," said the doctor, "does not mean that you are more likely to develop it."

Leukemia is not *contagious*. It cannot be spread from person to person like a cold. "Can I give it to my cat or dog?" Dave, age 11, wondered.

"No, you cannot pass it to an animal or another person," answered his doctor.

WARNING SIGNS

Ellie Murphy, age four, was usually very active. But for the last two weeks, she had been tired and pale, with dark circles under her eyes. Sometimes she ached all over.

Leukemia is not contagious. You cannot get it from associating with a person who has the disease.

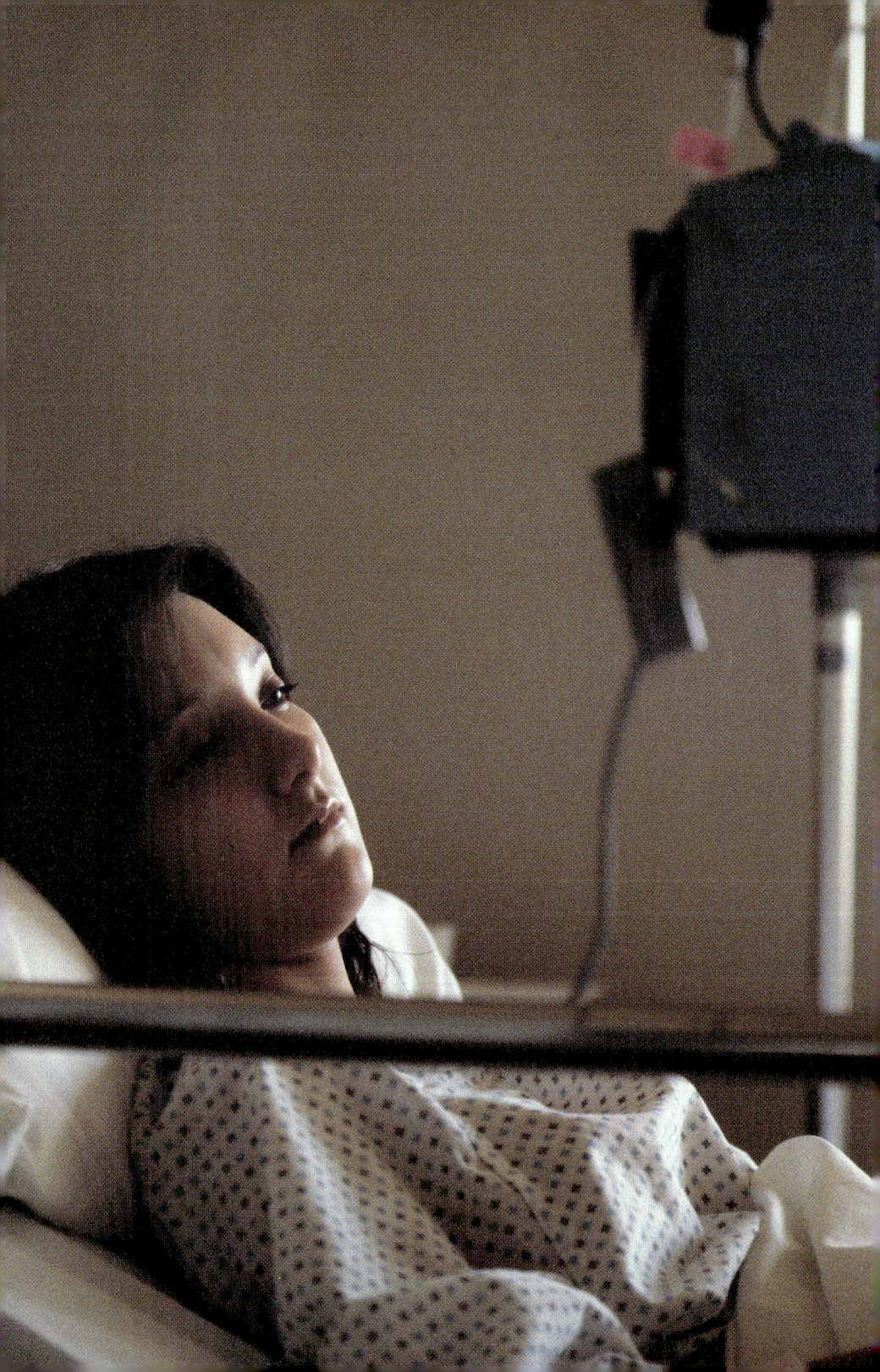

Maybe Ellie has the flu, thought her mother. But she was puzzled when Ellie's scraped knee would not heal. It kept bleeding a little, every day for a week.

Finally Mrs. Murphy brought Ellie to see Dr. Warner. After an examination and tests, Dr. Warner told Mr. and Mrs. Murphy that Ellie had leukemia. She had ALL. That is why the disease had come on so fast.

Ellie Murphy's early signs of leukemia are common ones. Many early symptoms are like those of a cold or flu. The symptoms sometimes change every day, so a trend may be hard to find. That is why the disease may be mistaken for something else.

ALL patients are often weak, tired, and pale, and they bruise easily. Like Ellie, their scrapes do not heal. They may run a fever and have nosebleeds and night sweats. Sometimes small red dots appear on their skin.

Rhonda, age 12, noticed that her clothes no longer fit. She had lost weight and caught colds easily. "My bones seem to ache," she told a friend. Once she went to the doctor, she found out why—she had leukemia.

If the disease is not treated, advanced symptoms develop. Leukemia patients may feel very tired and run high fevers. Their bone and joint aches may turn into more severe pain. Other symptoms include bleeding, swelling of the gums, and skin rashes.

Childhood chronic leukemia progresses more slowly. There are few early signs, so there is little warning of the disease. In fact, chronic leukemia may

People who have leukemia feel tired and worn out, and they may develop other symptoms like rashes and aching joints.

be present without any symptoms at all. The disease is often discovered when a patient goes to a doctor for another complaint. When symptoms do occur, they are like those of acute leukemia.

Patients may feel tired and weak. They start to lose weight because they do not feel hungry and do not eat enough. They may bruise and bleed easily and get frequent colds or flus. Fevers are common. Some patients may notice a general feeling of ill health or have night sweats or rashes.

In 1984 Anthony Hitchcock, 18 months old, developed a rash. The doctor thought the child was having an allergic reaction to laundry soap. Mrs. Hitchcock tried another brand. But the rash did not go away.

Next the doctor thought Anthony's bumps were a reaction to bug bites. He gave Mrs. Hitchcock a cream to put on the rash. Anthony's rash did not clear up. Instead it spread under his arms and on his chest and back.

Mrs. Hitchcock took Anthony back to the hospital. This time Anthony's doctor ran blood tests and told Mr. and Mrs. Hitchcock terrible news. Anthony had a very rare kind of chronic leukemia. Only about 60 cases are reported each year.

By then, Anthony had high fevers and had trouble breathing. The rash covered most of his body. He had dark circles under his eyes and was losing a lot of weight. Luckily, doctors were later able to *arrest*, or stop, his leukemia.

In Anthony's case, a rash was the only warning sign that something was wrong. You usually don't worry much about a rash. It may itch, but it goes away after a while.

However, Anthony's rash would not go away. This is the most important warning sign of leukemia—if a symptom lasts longer than a week or two, the person should see a doctor. Most children with symptoms that last awhile do not end up having diseases as serious as leukemia. But finding out for sure is important.

HARD TO DIAGNOSE

The warning signs of leukemia are often similar to those of common illnesses. So doctors need a lot of information before they can make a diagnosis. They get this information in several ways. First, they carefully examine their patients. If they think leukemia may be present, they do blood and bone marrow tests. These tests are the only ways to confirm leukemia.

Amy, age eight, went through these detection steps. She saw Dr. Smith because she felt tired and weak. She also had a fever, bone pain, and bruised easily. She felt too ill to play with her toys or friends. These symptoms had lasted two weeks.

After writing down her symptoms, Dr. Smith went over Amy's medical history. "Has Amy had mumps,

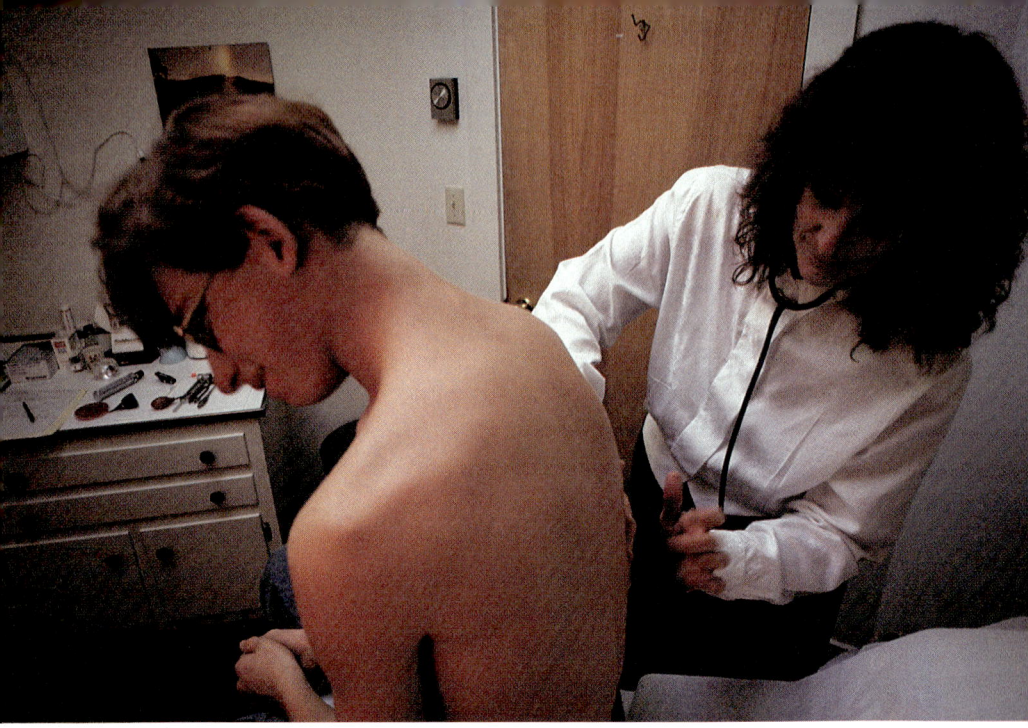

The first step in testing a patient for leukemia is a thorough medical examination.

measles, and chicken pox?" he asked her mother. "Has she been in the hospital before?" He took her blood pressure and pulse.

Then he examined Amy. He listened to her lungs and heart. He looked into her ears and eyes. Dr. Smith looked carefully at Amy's rash and the scraped knee that would not heal. He also found two large, fresh bruises. Amy's mother had no idea how she had gotten them. Finally, the doctor gently pressed on Amy's stomach and neck. Amy's liver, spleen, and lymph nodes were swollen.

Dr. Smith knew that these symptoms could mean different diagnoses. Amy could have a bad infection or *anemia*. Or she could have *rheumatic fever*, acute leukemia, or other cancers. To make a correct diagnosis, Dr. Smith needed blood tests.

He pricked one of Amy's fingers and took a little blood. Laboratory workers examined the blood under microscopes. They told Dr. Smith the number of platelets and white and red blood cells in Amy's blood. They also looked for leukemic cells but did not find any.

From these results, Dr. Smith narrowed Amy's disease to two choices. But he still could not make a definite diagnosis. So he went ahead with a bone marrow test.

He warned Amy, "This will hurt, but not for long." Dr. Smith decided to take a small amount of bone marrow from Amy's hip. Sometimes doctors use the breastbone. But in young people, the hip is used more often. This is because the hipbone is large and it is easier to remove bone marrow from it.

Dr. Smith used the *aspiration method* to draw out the bone marrow. He injected Amy's hip with an *anesthetic* to deaden the pain. Dr. Smith waited until Amy's hip was numb, then put a long needle through her skin to the top of her hip. He put a *syringe* on the needle and pulled back the syringe's plunger to suck Amy's red bone marrow into the syringe.

Laboratory workers then examined Amy's bone marrow under microscopes. They counted the number of platelets and red and white blood cells. The

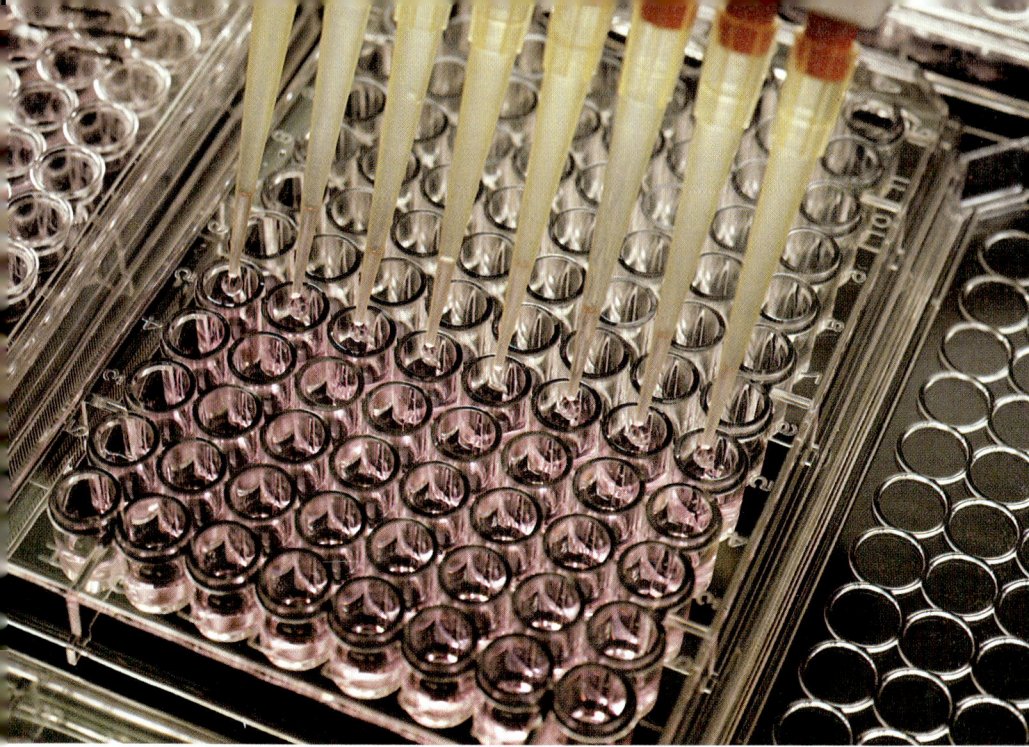

When doctors suspect that someone has leukemia, they run a series of blood tests to learn for certain.

numbers were not correct. They also looked for—and found—leukemic blasts. Now Dr. Smith knew Amy had acute lymphocytic leukemia—ALL.

TREATMENT

Treatment for leukemia begins right away. Patients receive the best and latest treatments in a medical center or hospital with a staff that specializes in leukemia treatment. There doctors, nurses, and other professionals work as a team to treat leukemia patients.

Chemotherapy is the most important treatment for leukemia. Doctors use combinations chosen from over 30 anticancer drugs to fight the disease. These drugs kill leukemic cells. Some kill leukemic cells directly. Others block the cells' ability to grow and multiply.

An *oncologist*, a doctor who treats cancers, gives anticancer drugs to patients. Oncologists know the right balance of anticancer drugs needed to destroy leukemic cells.

Some drugs are taken by mouth. Others are injected into a muscle or a vein. Once in the blood, an anticancer drug travels through the body. It reaches as many cancer cells as possible. How fast treatment works depends on the kind of anticancer drug and the kind of leukemia.

Anticancer drugs also damage normal, healthy cells. These powerful drugs can act on any fast-growing cells in the body. However, most normal cells soon recover after treatment ends.

The choice of anticancer drugs depends on the kind of leukemia and how far along it has progressed. Young people are often treated with several drugs. Leukemic cells that are not affected by one anticancer drug may be killed by others. In addition, drugs often work better together than they can alone. The individual patient also affects the rate at which treatment works. How healthy the patient is, his or her medical history, and other factors will all help determine the success of the treatment.

How often chemotherapy is given and how long it lasts varies. It depends on the kind of leukemia, the drugs used, and how the patients respond. Chemotherapy may be given each day, once a week, or once a month. Sometimes treatment is given on an on-and-off cycle that provides rest periods. This gives young patients a chance to build healthy new cells and regain their strength.

Some people have *side effects*, or uncomfortable reactions, to their anticancer drugs. The most common side effects are nausea, vomiting, hair loss, and feeling tired. Others include mouth sores and infections.

Sometimes doctors combine chemotherapy with other therapies such as surgery or *radiation therapy.* In radiation therapy, high-energy X rays kill leukemic cells. This treatment does little damage to normal cells.

Radiation may be beamed to the lymph nodes, the spleen, the spine, or the brain. Chemotherapy sometimes does not totally destroy the leukemic cells in these places.

Surgery is not often used. Doctors may remove the spleen in some kinds of leukemia.

Some leukemia patients get *bone marrow transplants.* This sounds like a type of surgery, but it is not. A bone marrow transplant is a *transfusion* of bone marrow.

Leukemia patients are given very large amounts of drugs or radiation to kill leukemic cells. However, these treatments kill too many healthy cells. The

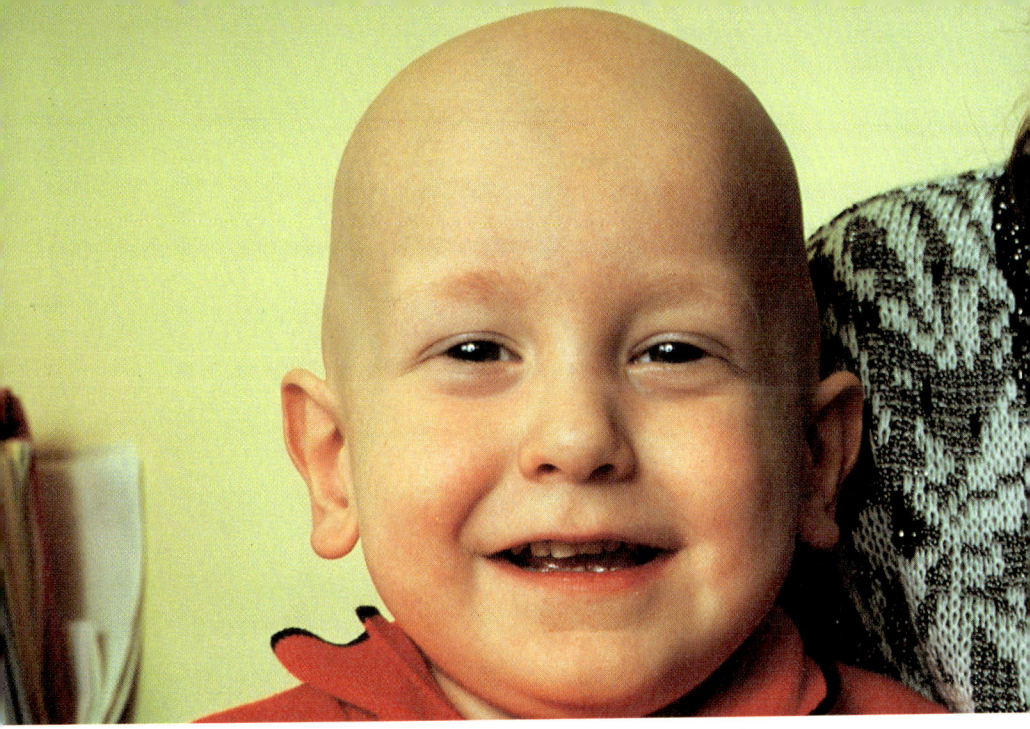

Anticancer drugs and radiation therapy may produce temporary side effects such as hair loss and weight gain.

bone marrow transplant restores the patient's bone marrow. It replaces the patient's bone marrow with healthy bone marrow from a donor. The patient's and donor's marrows must be a good match. If not, the donor's marrow is likely to react badly with the patient's organs and tissues.

Today bone marrow transplant is an important method to treat some leukemia patients. It is used on patients who do not respond well to chemotherapy or who get leukemia again. About 1,200 bone marrow transplants for leukemia were done in the United States in 1989. This number includes both children and adults.

SUPPORTIVE THERAPY

Supportive therapy protects leukemia patients from infections or other diseases. It helps keep them strong. As leukemia progresses, the number of normal blood cells drop. Anticancer drugs may damage or slow down production of healthy blood cells even more. So leukemia patients often have more infections, anemia, and bleeding.

Supportive treatments help fight these conditions. They maintain patients until the benefits of chemotherapy or radiation can take effect. There are a variety of supportive therapies, and sometimes they are combined.

Most young people need transfusions of cells. Transfusions of red blood cells help supply enough oxygen to their body. White blood cell transfusions help them fight infections. Platelet transfusions allow patients to clot after an injury.

At the first sign of an infection, patients get *antibiotics*. These drugs help fight infections. The treatments used to cure leukemia lower the body's resistance to disease. Common infections, such as colds, become serious threats to leukemia patients.

Sometimes patients are put into germ-free, isolation rooms. These rooms reduce exposure to infections. This is done when the patients are very weak or after bone marrow transplants.

Leukemia patients must be watched carefully, as the drugs they take make them susceptible to infections.

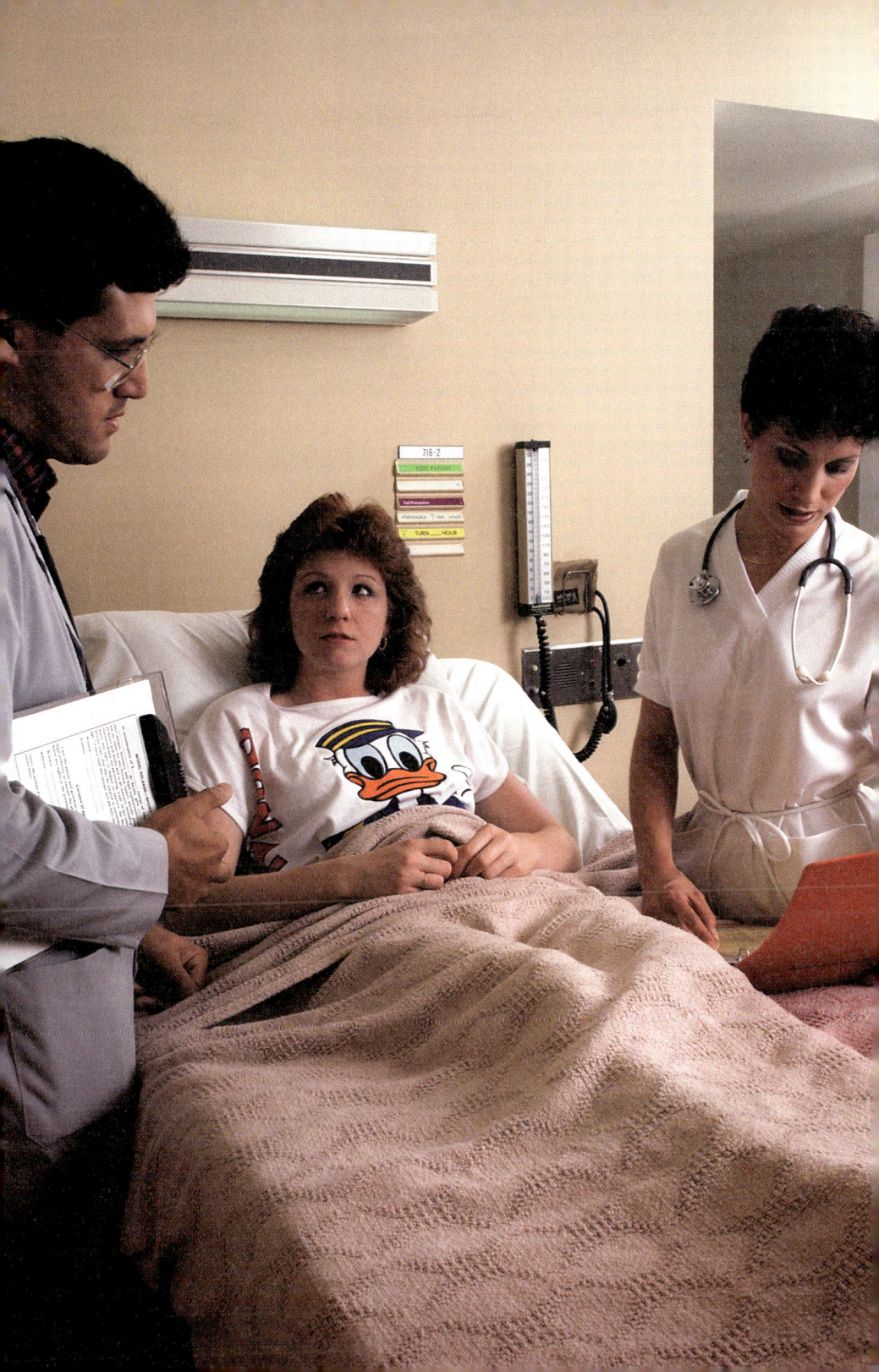

TODD'S STORY

Todd, age 11, was diagnosed with ALL. His parents checked him into a nearby cancer hospital. Oncologists started Todd on three drugs right away. The drugs would fight his leukemia in three ways.

"You'll probably have side effects from the drugs," the oncologists told him. "We don't know which ones you'll have, though. Keep telling us how you feel."

Because anticancer drugs are so powerful, their side effects can be serious. The drugs also affect normal cells. The oncologists watched Todd for side effects and to see how the treatment was working.

Todd took *prednisone* pills every day. This drug is a natural body chemical. Prednisone stops leukemic blasts from growing, but it can also make people hungry. Todd gained weight and became fat.

Once a week, Todd had injections of a drug called *vincristine*. It is made from a common flower, the periwinkle. This drug stops cancer cells from multiplying. Vincristine gave Todd stomach cramps. His fingers and toes often tingled and hurt. What he hated the most, though, were the mouth and lip sores the drug caused.

The third drug on Todd's list was *daunorubicin*. This drug helped him fight off infections. He got injections every three weeks. The drug made him vomit. He also lost his hair.

Todd's oncologists worried that leukemic cells remained in his brain. Chemotherapy was killing the blasts in his blood and bone marrow. But the brain has a built-in barrier to keep out drugs.

To kill leukemic cells in Todd's brain, oncologists did two things. First, they injected a drug called *methotrexate* into his spine. The spine carries drugs directly into the brain. Todd also had radiation therapy to kill any remaining leukemic cells. After these radiation sessions, Todd often got a headache and vomited.

After a few months, Todd's oncologists had good news. "Your leukemia has disappeared. You're in *remission* and can go home!" Todd was free from any signs of leukemia. Many young people are in remission after only four weeks of chemotherapy.

Todd then began long-term treatment at home. He took methotrexate pills and other anticancer drugs every week to keep his leukemia from coming back. He often went to the hospital for checkups. Todd continued this treatment for more than two years. He is still in remission and has stopped chemotherapy. His hair has grown back and he has slimmed down. Today he feels fine.

Like Todd, most young people stay on long-term treatment for two and a half to three years. During this time, oncologists give them combinations of anticancer drugs to extend and maintain remission.

AFTER TREATMENT

Doctors discharge leukemia patients from the hospital as soon as possible after treatment. It is important for young people to lead normal lives. Most feel well enough to resume many of their usual activities.

Oncologists stress not to limit activities. Jane's doctor told her, "Go to school. Play with your friends. Go back to your dancing lessons. If you feel tired, slow down or stop."

Doctors recommend that leukemia patients resume their normal activities as soon as possible after leaving the hospital.

Doctors also tell families to use the same rules for all their children. "Don't baby Tim because he has leukemia," warned the oncologist. "If he disobeys, punish him. Don't shower him with gifts. Your other children will resent all that attention."

When Lori, age 11, came home from the hospital, she told her three brothers she could get anything she wanted. "You can't touch me. If you do, I'll bleed to death, and it'll be your fault!"

Lori's mother heard about this. "Lori, you are not a privileged member of this family. You have duties and chores around here, just like your brothers," she told her daughter.

Lori's mother knew it was important that all her children obey the same family rules. She did not want Lori to become spoiled and demanding. The boys would soon resent Lori if she got her way all the time.

Some children, though, do need special care. They need to understand this, so they do not think they are being punished. Bob, age nine, had been home for three months after his initial leukemia treatment. One day, he vomited and said his stomach hurt. His temperature was 103. He went back to the hospital.

Bob was scared. He asked his doctor, "Why am I back? Did I do something bad?"

His doctor said, "No, you didn't do anything bad. We have to find out why you don't feel well. You'll have to stay in the hospital for a while. We want to help you feel better."

With good diets and proper medication, most leukemia patients can participate in sports without any risk to their health.

Sometimes parents try to overprotect their children who have leukemia. They expect these children to follow strict rules. Tyler, age 11, feels his parents overprotect him. "They tell me I can't do anything that might tire me out. I can't play baseball with my friends. Or wrestle with my younger brother. My parents think I might get hurt."

Other children in the family need to know what is wrong with their brother or sister. Doctors recommend that parents give honest answers to questions. Leukemia is not just a cold—it is a serious disease. When children understand about leukemia, they are less likely to resent special treatment of the ill child.

Once at home, children with leukemia will have blood tests two to four times a month. They will also have bone marrow tests, but not as often. They will continue taking anticancer drugs and antibiotics. Doctors recommend a good diet, with lots of bread, fruits, and vegetables. And they tell their patients to continue normal activities, friendships, and being part of their family activities. But they should tell their doctor right away if a sister, brother, or playmate comes down with chicken pox.

IN REMISSION

Elena Chiesa, age 11, had ALL. After her initial chemotherapy, she went into remission. But after 18 months, Elena had a bone marrow *relapse*. This meant that the leukemia had grown back in her bone marrow.

A relapse is bad news. It often means that the leukemic cells have become resistant to the drugs. It also means that a cure is less likely.

Elena went back to the hospital and received large amounts of new anticancer drugs. All over again, she lost her hair, put on weight, and had other side effects. Then she went back on long-term treatment.

The second treatment was worth it. After two years, her leukemia again went into remission. This time she stayed well.

Today Elena is 19 and a college student. Doctors say

she has a good chance of living a long, healthy life. "I feel great," says Elena, "but I'm very lucky."

Many leukemia patients in remission feel like Elena. One 15-year-old said, "The thing I'm most happy about is that I'm alive. I appreciate life more than I did before."

Some patients worry that they may not spot signs of a relapse. They need not worry. Their regular blood and bone marrow tests will show if this is happening. A relapse often shows up in the bone marrow before it is found in the blood.

However, some symptoms may appear between regular checkups and tests. Doctors should be told right away of bleeding that will not stop, bone or joint pain, or paleness. They also need to know if the patient bruises easily, has night sweats, or has trouble breathing.

Treatment after a relapse often does not last as long as the initial treatment. But after the first relapse, any other relapses are harder to control.

A POSITIVE OUTLOOK

Twenty years ago, doctors had no good leukemia treatments. Most young people with leukemia lived a year or less after diagnosis. Only 25 percent, or one out of four, had remissions.

Today more than 90 percent of children with ALL go into remission. About 65 percent stay in remission

Today, more so than ever before, children with leukemia have a better chance to live long, healthy lives.

more than five years. After five years of remission, they are considered cured.

Why do young patients do so well today? In the past, oncologists gave patients one anticancer drug at a time. Then they found that two or more drugs together gave better results.

Before, doctors did not know that steady treatment over a period of time did not work as well as more aggressive therapy. Now they give very high amounts of anticancer drugs right after the diagnosis. It is best to kill leukemic cells as soon as possible.

Children with leukemia are easier to treat than adults with the disease.

Finally, doctors used to stop treatment once patients went into remission. Doctors now continue treatment for two to three years, even if they cannot find any leukemic blasts. If they stop too soon, children may relapse.

Doctors have had more success in treating leukemic children than adults. Most young people do not have any other major diseases. Adults may have heart disease, diabetes, or lung problems in addition to leukemia. So children fight only one disease at a time. Also, side effects are often less severe in children than in adults. Elena Chiesa, for example, had chemotherapy every Thursday. By Friday evening, she was often well enough to go roller-skating with her friends.

HELP FOR LEUKEMIA PATIENTS

In the United States, more than 80 major medical centers specialize in cancer. Some are specifically for leukemia and some are especially for children.

Most of these centers also do leukemia research. Researchers look for more effective drugs and treatments for leukemia patients. They exchange information on their findings. About 40 other cancer centers research new treatments, too.

The National Cancer Institute (NCI) has a list of all cancer research and medical centers. The NCI is a federal organization that provides many services. Its Office of Cancer Communications sends out information on research and patient services. The NCI also helps support cancer research centers and runs a special cancer treatment center in Bethesda, Maryland.

The NCI's treatment center is not a regular hospital. It is a research center where new treatments are developed and tested. Oncologists at the center do many kinds of studies.

The center takes only patients who are referred from other doctors. Patients accepted to one of its studies are treated at no cost.

Three national cancer organizations also help leukemia patients. The Leukemia Society of America has 57 chapters across America. This agency helps families pay for the high cost of leukemia treatment and also assists them in finding other ways to obtain funds.

The Candlelighters is an international organization of parents whose children have or have had cancer, including leukemia. The Candlelighters' network includes more than 300 groups around the world. Members exchange medical and practical information and give support to each other. The organization also helps families find counseling services.

Probably the best-known national organization is the American Cancer Society. It has programs in

40 *Several medical centers in the United States specialize in looking for new treatments—and a cure—for leukemia.*

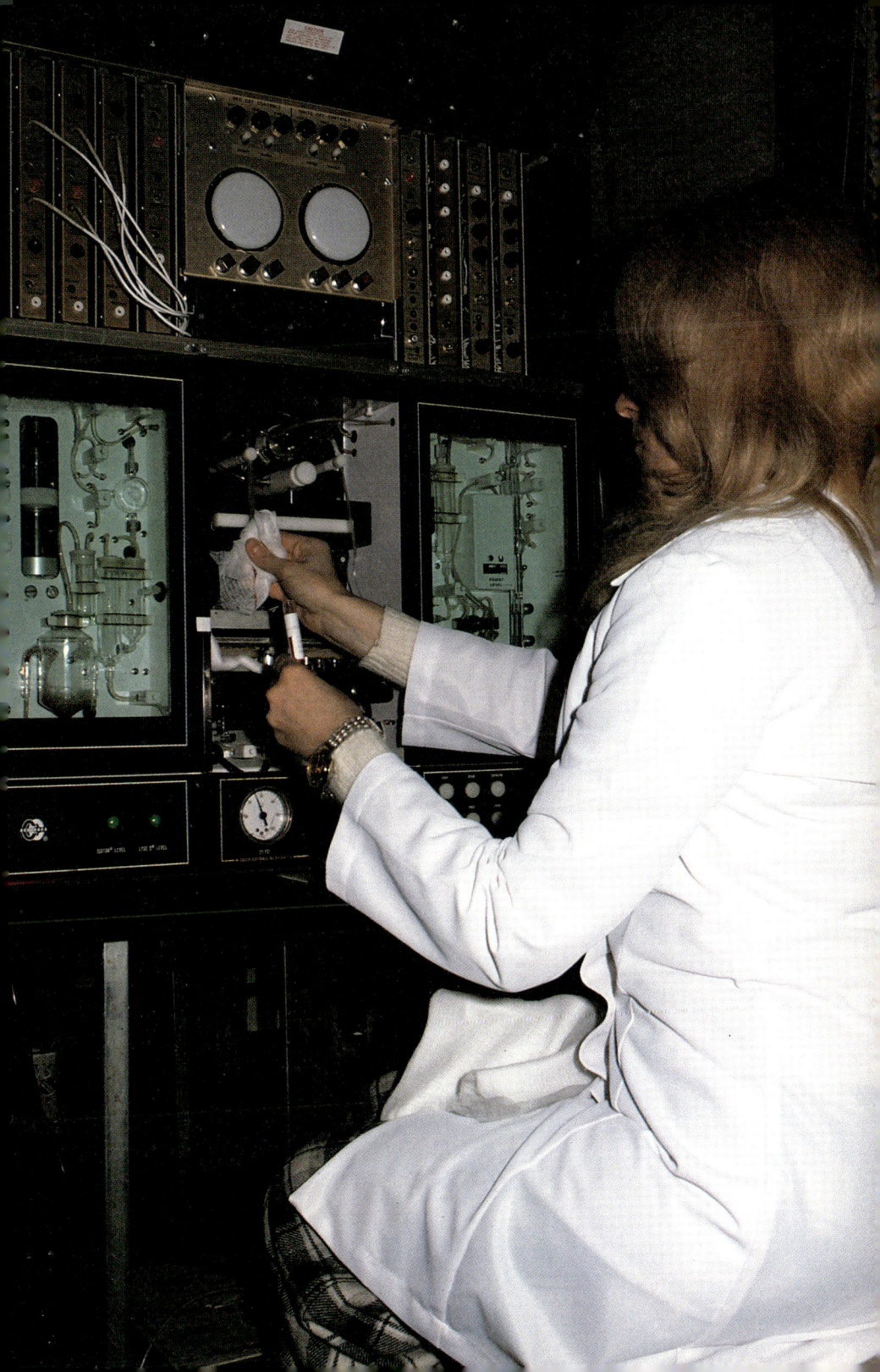

cancer research, education, and patient services. Local chapters across the United States raise money to support these programs.

The American Cancer Society and the National Cancer Institute sponsor a national network of cancer help centers. Callers can use a toll-free 800 number, or they can call their local American Cancer Society chapter. You can get a lot of information from this phone call—medical information, where the nearest medical treatment centers and treatment programs are, home-care help, and counseling referrals.

HOPE FOR THE FUTURE

Every day four kinds of leukemia research go on across the United States. One kind of research looks at what makes leukemic cells form. Researchers want to know how leukemia cells differ from normal cells.

A second kind of research focuses on why people get leukemia. Researchers are looking into four possible causes—viruses, chemicals, radiation, and defects in body chemistry. A third research area is *immunology*. This is the study of the body's natural defense system. Researchers want to know if leukemia occurs because of a defect in this system. Someday they hope to boost the body's natural defenses against leukemia.

Finally, researchers are developing new leukemia treatments. Doctors want safer and faster-acting drugs. They want the new drugs to kill leukemic cells without damaging normal cells. Researchers are also trying to find better supportive therapy methods.

Since the 1970s, research has resulted in new and better drugs for treating leukemia patients. Today's treatments mean that many young patients will have long, normal lives. Continuing research holds hope for longer life, and a cure, for all those with leukemia.

FOR MORE INFORMATION

The National Cancer Institute
1-800-4-CANCER

American Cancer Society
90 Park Avenue
New York, NY 10016
Look in your telephone book for a local chapter.

The Candlelighters
Childhood Cancer Foundation
1312 18th Street NW, 2nd floor
Washington, DC 20036

Leukemia Society of America
733 Third Avenue
New York, NY 10017

The National Leukemia Association, Inc.
585 Stewart Avenue
Suite 536
Garden City, NY 11530

GLOSSARY/INDEX

ACUTE 13—*Something that happens quickly or over a short period of time.*
ACUTE LYMPHOCYTIC LEUKEMIA 13, 24, 30, 35, 36—*The most common kind of childhood leukemia. It is also called ALL.*
ANEMIA 23, 28—*A condition in which there are not enough red blood cells in the blood.*
ANESTHETIC 23—*A drug that deadens pain.*
ANTIBIOTICS 28, 35—*Drugs that help fight infections.*
ANTICANCER DRUGS 5, 15, 25, 26, 30, 31, 35, 38—*Drugs that fight cancer.*
ARREST 20—*To stop a disease where it is, so it does not progress any further.*
ASPIRATION METHOD 23—*A method to draw out bone marrow from the body.*
BACTERIA 10—*Very tiny plants. Bacteria are so small that they can be seen only through a microscope. Some kinds of bacteria cause diseases. Other kinds do useful things.*
BLAST 10, 11, 24, 30, 31, 39—*Short name for lymphoblast. Blasts are young, immature white blood cells.*
BONE MARROW 9–13, 23, 26, 27, 31, 35, 36—*A jellylike substance that fills the insides of bones. Many blood cells are made here.*

BONE MARROW TRANSPLANT 26–28—*A procedure in which a patient's unhealthy bone marrow is replaced with new bone marrow from a donor.*
CANCER 5, 8, 23, 39, 40, 42—*A disease in which some cells of the body grow too fast and destroy healthy tissues and organs.*
CHEMOTHERAPY 5, 26–28, 31, 35, 39—*The use of drugs to treat disease.*
CHRONIC 13, 14, 19—*A term to describe a disease that progresses slowly.*
CONTAGIOUS 16—*Spread from person to person.*
DAUNORUBICIN 30—*An anticancer drug that helps fight infections.*
DIAGNOSIS 6, 36, 38—*The identification of a disease based on its signs and symptoms.*
IMMUNOLOGY 42—*The study of the body's natural defense system.*
INHERIT 16—*To get from one's parents.*
LYMPHATIC SYSTEM 9—*The network of small vessels that carry fluid between the tissues of the body and the bloodstream. This fluid washes the tissues and keeps them healthy.*
LYMPH NODES 10, 22, 26—*Bean-shaped structures scattered along vessels of the lymphatic system. The nodes act as filters, collecting foreign material or cancer cells that may travel through the lymphatic system.*
LYMPHOBLASTS 10—*Young, immature white blood cells. Called blasts for short.*

LYMPHOCYTES 10, 13—*White blood cells that make substances to fight foreign materials.*
METHOTREXATE 31—*An anticancer drug that kills cancer cells.*
MICROSCOPE 8, 11, 23—*An instrument that enlarges or magnifies objects.*
MONOCYTES 10, 13—*White blood cells that destroy foreign materials.*
NEUTROPHILS 10, 13, 14—*White blood cells that "eat" bacteria.*
ONCOLOGIST 25, 30, 31, 33, 38, 40—*A doctor who treats cancer.*
PLATELETS 10, 23, 28—*Blood cells that help stop bleeding.*
PREDNISONE 30—*An anticancer drug that stops leukemic cells from growing.*
RADIATION THERAPY 26, 31—*Treatment using high-energy X rays to destroy cancer.*
RED BLOOD CELLS 10, 11, 23—*Blood cells that carry oxygen through the body and remove carbon dioxide and other waste.*
RELAPSE 35, 36, 39—*When a disease comes back after a period of no symptoms.*
REMISSION 31, 35, 36, 39—*Free from any cancer symptoms.*
RHEUMATIC FEVER 23—*A disease in which joints and the heart valves become inflamed and the patient runs a high fever. It mostly afflicts young adults and children.*

47

SIDE EFFECTS 26, 30, 35—*Uncomfortable reactions to a drug.*

SPLEEN 10, 26—*An organ near the stomach that filters out foreign materials and cancer cells. In leukemia patients it often becomes enlarged.*

SUPPORTIVE THERAPY 28—*Treatment to protect leukemia patients from other diseases as they go through chemotherapy or radiation therapy.*

SYRINGE 23—*A device used to inject liquids into the body or to draw liquids out of the body. A syringe has a hollow barrel fitted with a plunger and a hollow needle.*

TRANSFUSION 26, 28—*The transfer of liquids from one person to another.*

VINCRISTINE 30—*An anticancer drug that stops cancer cells from multiplying.*

VIRUS 14, 42—*A tiny organism that causes disease.*

WHITE BLOOD CELLS 8, 10–13, 23, 28—*The blood cells that fight infections. There are three kinds of white blood cells: lymphocytes, monocytes, and neutrophils.*

ABD-4033

ABE-3749